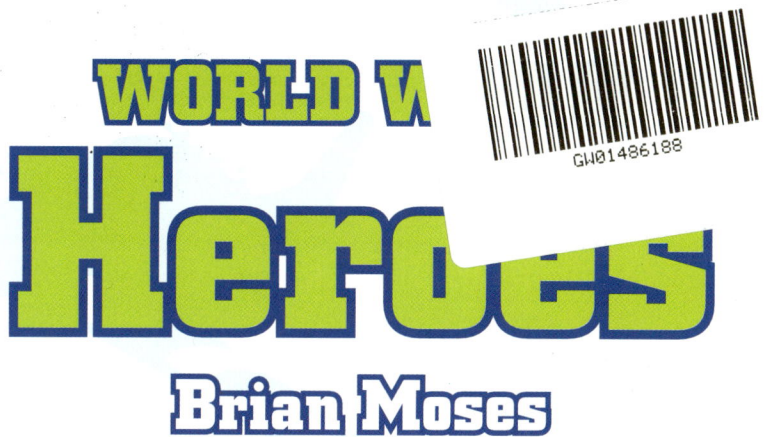

World War Heroes
Brian Moses

Contents

Douglas Bader	3
Leonard Cheshire	9
Guy Gibson	11
Nancy Wake	15
Violette Szabo	18
Roger Bushell	20
Witold Pilecki	22
Margot Turner	26

Heroes inspire all of us. They are people who refuse to admit that they're beaten even when everything seems stacked against them. In this book you can read about eight such heroes.

Douglas Bader

Douglas Bader had been a pilot officer for only eighteen months when he crashed his plane and was badly hurt. The accident led to the loss of both his legs. Gradually he learnt to walk again on artificial legs. He was even able to fly again, but the RAF decided that he should retire due to his ill-health.

When war broke out, Bader was determined to get back into the RAF and fly again. He was passed fit by a medical board. In June 1940 he found himself in charge of a Canadian squadron where the pilots had lost all enthusiasm for fighting. Bader, the flying ace with tin legs, was an inspiration to these men.

In July 1940, at the start of the Battle of Britain, Bader shot down his first enemy plane. Twenty more were to follow over the next year. The pilots who flew with Bader saw him as "the bravest of the brave".

Bader's own luck ran out in August 1941. He was chasing enemy aircraft over France when one of them hit his plane. It broke in two. Bader struggled to free himself from the plane as it plunged towards the ground, but one of his legs became trapped. As he pulled harder his leg came away. He was now clear of the plane and able to open his parachute.

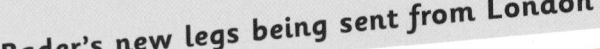
Bader's new legs being sent from London

Bader asked the Germans who captured him if they would search for his missing leg, and also send for a spare one from England. They agreed to both requests. Bader then escaped from a German hospital but was recaptured. He spent time in a number of prisoner-of-war camps before being sent to Colditz Castle.

Bader soon realised that escape from Colditz was impossible. He spent the rest of the war making life as difficult as he could for the soldiers guarding the castle – even if it meant harsh punishment in return. He was finally rescued by American troops in April 1945.

Leonard Cheshire

Leonard Cheshire was another hero of the skies in World War II. Cheshire flew bombers and his planes were often covered in gashes and holes where he had been shot. In spite of this, he was never injured himself.

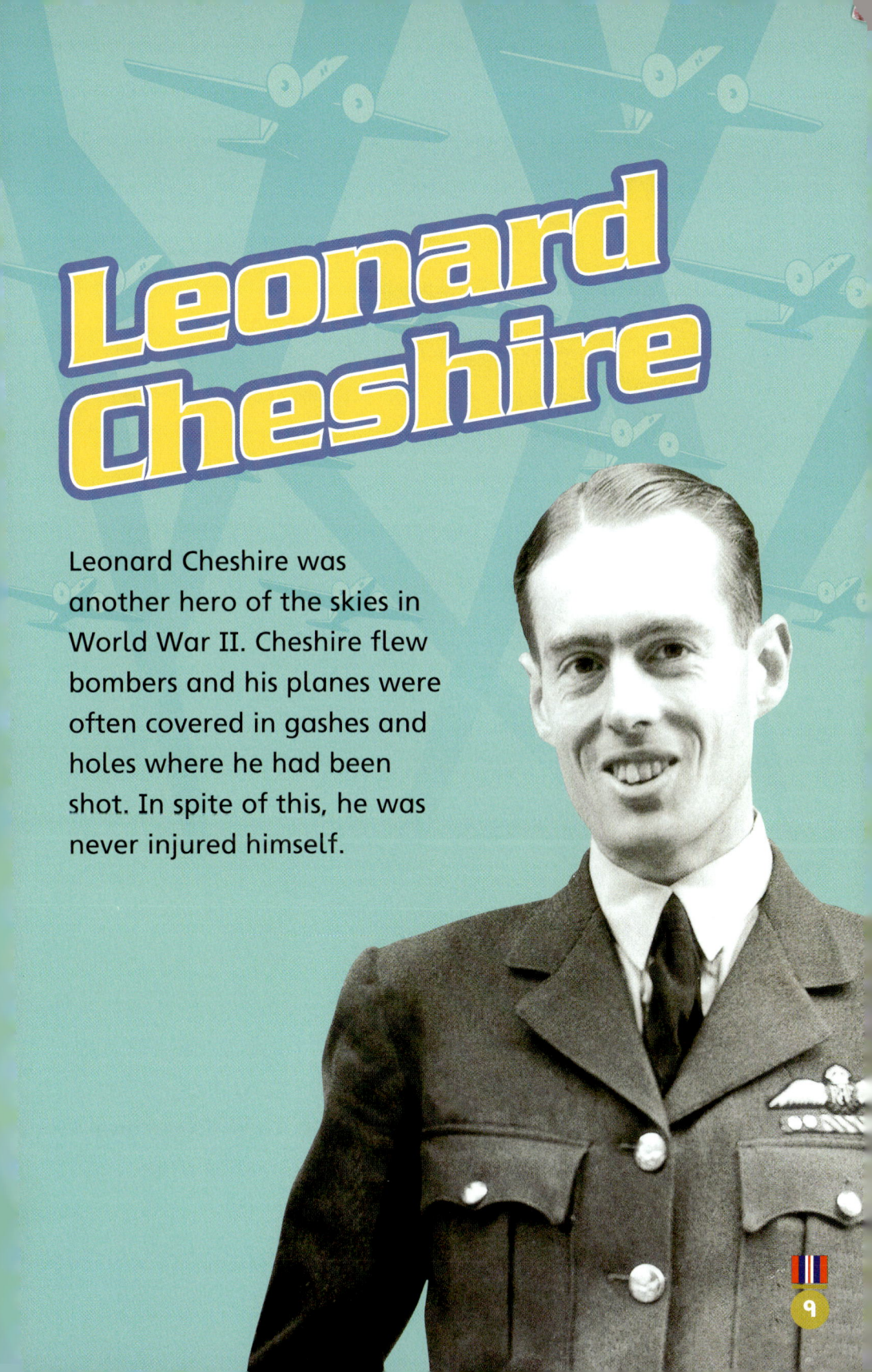

In 1944 Cheshire was awarded the Victoria Cross (VC) medal, which is usually given for a single act of bravery. Cheshire was given his medal for the courage he had shown during more than one hundred bombing raids over Germany.

Guy Gibson

Guy Gibsonly Gibson was asked to put together a new squadron to take part in a dangerous raid on the Mohne and Eder dams in the heart of Germany.

Gibson learnt that his planes would be carrying an amazing new weapon – the bouncing bomb. This was a bomb that needed to be dropped from a very low height so that it would bounce on water like a skimmed stone.

After two months of preparation the attack took place. The first bomb failed to blow open the Mohne dam and the second plane was shot down. As the other aircraft flew in to drop their bombs Gibson flew his plane alongside each of them in turn, to try to protect them from enemy fire. Finally the dam was broken and they moved on to attack the second dam.

The raid was a success but at a high price. Many planes were lost and over 50 airmen were killed. Gibson spent the next three days writing personal letters to their families. He won the VC for his own bravery in the raid.

Nancy Wake

Nancy Wake was born in Australia. In the early 1930s she moved to France where she worked as a journalist in Paris. She loved living in France and married a Frenchman. When the Germans invaded France in 1940, their house became a 'safe house' where people could hide if the Germans were looking for them.

Nancy Wake also travelled throughout France taking messages that were important in the struggle against the Germans. She was part of a network of people who helped over a thousand men to escape from France. Her code name was the "White Mouse".

With the Germans after her, Nancy Wake fled to England. She was trained as a secret agent. In 1944 she parachuted back into France where she led raids on German factories. She was never captured although, sadly, her husband was killed by the Germans in an attempt to make the White Mouse give herself up.

Violette Szabo

Violette Szabo was also parachuted into France. Her mission was to help delay the German army as it moved north to block the D-Day invasion. She was working with another freedom fighter called Anastasie when they were both ambushed by the Germans. They fled, but Violette injured her ankle and couldn't run any further.

Violette forced Anastasie to go on alone and then began firing at the Germans. She kept them pinned down until her gun was empty of bullets and the Germans were able to capture her. She was executed just a few days before the end of the war.

Roger Bushell

"If you escape again, we will shoot you." This was what Squadron Leader Roger Bushell was told after he had made several escape attempts from German prisoner-of-war camps. Most people would have sat back and waited for the war to finish, but not Roger Bushell.

A scene from the film *The Great Escape*

Bushell was in charge of an escape plan to free 200 prisoners from the prison camp of Stalag Luft III. Three tunnels were begun and nicknamed "Tom, Dick and Harry". Tom was discovered very quickly. Dick was then used as a store tunnel until Harry was finally finished.

Everything went wrong on the night set for the escape. A total of 76 men made it through the tunnel, but only three managed to escape from Germany. The Germans kept their word and shot Bushell along with 50 others. The film *The Great Escape* was inspired by this event.

Witold Pilecki

Witold Pilecki was a Polish army officer. He was married with a daughter but, for him, his country had to come before his family. Many Poles were being sent to German prison camps and Pilecki needed to find out just how bad they were. So he got himself arrested and was sent to the newly-built camp at Auschwitz.

Conditions at the camp were worse than Pilecki had thought. He almost died in the first few weeks, but then got better and was able to smuggle out messages.
He set up leaders among the prisoners and was able to arrange some escapes.

After three terrible years at the camp it became far too dangerous for Pilecki to stay there any longer. He managed to escape himself, but found that few people believed or wanted to believe what was really happening in the Nazi death camps.

Margot Turner

In early 1942 Margot Turner was a nurse in Malaya. The Japanese bombed the capital, Kuala Lumpur, and her patients were moved to Singapore. The order was given for all nurses to be evacuated by boat.

The boat that Margot Turner sailed on was bombed by the Japanese but she was able to swim ashore. She was picked up by another ship and carried on nursing the wounded. The second ship was also bombed and Margot found herself back in the water.

Margot and her friend Beatrice got hold of two life rafts which they tied together. Of the fourteen women and children on the life rafts only Margot survived the many days at sea. Almost dead from the effects of the hot sun, she was saved by the doctor on a Japanese ship.

She then survived the most awful conditions in Japanese prison camps for nearly three years, almost dying on one occasion. Her story showed the world that women have the strength and courage to survive terrible hardship. She was awarded the MBE in 1946.

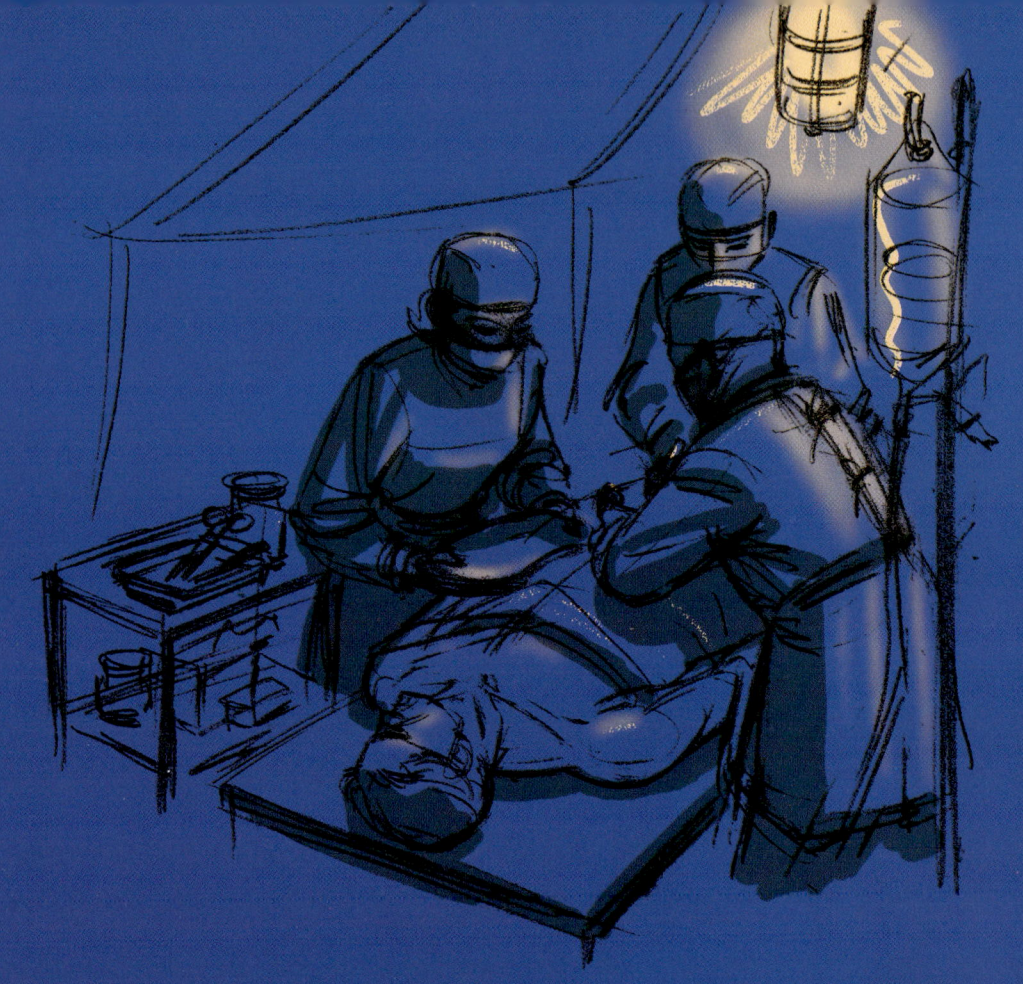

There were, of course, many more heroes in World War II. There were those who received medals for their brave deeds, and there were others who risked their lives almost daily to help others. There were nurses and doctors who tended the wounded while a battle raged around them. There were bomb disposal experts where one false move could signal disaster, and there were firefighters who entered blazing buildings to rescue those trapped inside.

Heroes are modest people. They make light of what they do. In the words of the White Mouse:

"I may have lost a lot in the war – but I made a lot of friends and I did what I felt I had to do. And plenty of other people lost more, or did more, than I ever did."

Acknowledgements

We are grateful to the following for permission to reproduce copyright photographs:

Mary Evans Picture Library page 22; Ronald Grant Archive page 20-21; Hulton Archive pages 9, 14, 15, 26; Magnum Photos page 24-25; Popperfoto pages 2, 3, 6, 7, 10, 11, 23, 27; Topham Picturepoint pages 8, 13.

Front cover: Hulton Archive
Back cover: Popperfoto